MW00606324

Office Poetry ©

by

Robert Petta

Illustrated by

Mark Sean Wilson

Conner,
I appreciate
very much your likeness
in this book & your dad's
and more my young
Jedi!

1

Office Poetry(c)
By
Robert Petta

Published by:
Light Underground Publishing
P.O. Box 270249
Austin, TX 78727

ISBN, 1st print edition: 978-0-9795585-0-4
First printing September 2007
Library of Congress Control Number: 2007904033

Office Poetry ©

Table of Contents

Preface
Dedications

Office Poetry ©

Office Poetry ©

This book is dedicated to all the honorable men and women of the labor force around the globe.

Poetry doesn't belong to those who write it,
but to those who need it.
- Author Unknown

And for my beloved Stephanie

Office Poetry

Staring at
a computer screen,
fielding tons of calls;
slaving for a company,
languishing within its walls;
beaten by the drudgery
of monotonous tasks and skills;
frittering away your precious time,
dragging through the drills.

I tried to block it out
with good thoughts, church, and beer.
I just can't sit around and pout
because losing my house I fear.
I long, like you, to stand and shout,
"I quit! I won the lottery!"
Or "I'm starting my own business
selling artwork and pottery!"
Or "I am moving
to Hawaii,
or Mexico or Tahiti;"
or "I just got
a huge inheritance
from someone in my family."
Or "I am starting a commune
in a desert near Santa Fe;"
or "I just got the main lead part
in a hit musical on Broadway."

Whatever your fortunes and dreams,
whatever your heart desires,
whatever your plans and schemes,
whatever may light your fires,
whatever you may do,
wherever you may work,
these poems are for you,
to provide a laugh or smirk.

Just at that time you feel
you're locked within a cage,
or spinning on a wheel,
or feeling some pent up rage;
or drowning in dismay,
or a sinking in your gut,
or your attitude decay,
or stuck in some deep rut;

just take this book in hand
and start to read one poem;
it will take you to a land,
where your cares and dreams can roam.
We'll hunt anger down with laughter
and shoot phrases laced with venom;
we'll wring out all our bitter words
and make lemonade from lemons.

I've taken the liberty,
while working on the clock,
to compose some poetry
and spring our mental lock.
To help stop the wheel from spinning,
to relieve us from this craze,
to break up the routine,
and free us from this maze.
So take a look around-
now take a second look.
For laughter can be found
where you work and in this book.

So come experience a work related rhyme;
drift off and be at bliss, while still on company time.
Take a break from the rat race,
break free from the company's chains.
Office Poetry will put a smile on your face;
Office Poetry is candy for your brains.

Parking Space

The hunt begins at 7:45,
when the early employees start to arrive,
through the lot and garage they all must race,
to claim their trophy parking space.

All of their minds are determined and set.
They'll give no quarter and none you will get.
They circle the lot like wolves on the prowl.
Their faces contorted into a menacing scowl.

Their fuel, the primal rule, first come first serve.
No pity for latecomers and none they deserve.
The ones in the front are ravaged first.
Just five minutes late and you'll get the worst.

Enterprising sorts won't search the whole lot;
they'll fake a bum knee to get a handicap spot,
grumbling to you as they pretend to limp along,
"Just three more months, and this pain should be gone."

A rush of excitement, a stroke of luck!
You spot one near the front by a truck.
You're set to pounce, no handicap marked.
But in it you find a motorcycle parked.

They've cut the size to squeeze in more.
Now SUV owners must squirm through their doors.
And one week's paycheck has to be spent,
repairing your car from door-dings or dents.

We'll work like mules to win an award,
that places our name up on a board,
reserving our spot by the CEO,
and those who poach shall pay for their tow.

When noon arrives it creates a new crunch
as hungry employees exit the lot for their lunch.
But incoming traffic from the late-shift crew
creates another struggle for the vacated few.

Beware of the space that has the storm drain,
its steep crevasse has caused ankles to sprain.
And the ones under trees with the shade are a trap,
they'll take perfectly clean cars and cover them bird crap.

Right in front there are spaces for guests.
The temptation is fierce; we know they're the best.
But on the days when it happens to rain,
all rules are off; we'll park in the fire lane!

We know we're all working for the grand promotion,
to be granted a reserved spot, and avoid all the commotion.
But until that glorious day doth arrive,
we'll continue to hunt! Only the strong will survive.

ID Badge

To my corpus it's always tethered,
like some military dog tag.
It is the key to my employment,
it is my ID badge.

Too often have I arrived at work
my stomach in a knot,
although I remembered to grab my lunch,
this tool to enter I had forgot.

My smiling face displayed to all
as I make departmental rounds.
I just wish that when this picture was taken
I could have shed about forty pounds.

It has been washed and dried and washed again
when I have left it in my pants.
Every time I use the magnetic strip
it's a game of random chance.

And yet it's like a human sometimes
in the sense that it has its moods.
It will fail you twenty times in a row,
but on the twenty first, it will go right through.

And as you stand there swiping it
time and time again,
no one's allowed to just let you in,
not even your best friend.

It's amazing how it always knows
me from all the others.
The mystery is the secret code;
it can differentiate identical twin brothers.

On the back it has instructions
if it's ever lost or misplaced.
But having to have a temporary one issued
leaves you feeling like some sort of disgrace.

So if I'm ever in a wreck,
or meet with some horrendous fate,
please quickly check my ID badge
and call work to say I'll be late.

Elevator Ride

The debate occurs
at every floor;
just how long
do you hold the door?

Coffee cup in hand,
a pep in their gait,
you see them coming,
but know they must wait.

The look in their eyes
as the doors close shut
stirs up a feeling
deep down in your gut.

It seems so brutal
when you're running late,
pressing the button,
and sealing their fate.

You know it's wrong,
you feel empathy;
so your futile try
to hold it they'll see.

There is a reason,
but to us unknown,
why people prefer
to ride it alone.

I guess it's the fear
that won't go away
of trying to think
of something to say.

After "good morning,"
your mind starts to search
for the next topic
as you feel the lurch.

The pressure intense
as the floors go by.
To break the silence
you let out a sigh.

"Nice weather we have,"
you blurt with a strain,
before you notice
she's covered in rain.

So feeling awkward
you guess at her name.
But getting that wrong
now deepens your shame.

Off to a bad start
and just getting worse.
You sense in her fear
by her grip on her purse.

You must say something
to just break the ice.
Fumbling around
you say, "You look nice."

"Thank you," her reply,
"I'll tell my husband."
Attempts at small talk
have failed you again.

You say as she leaves,
"I'll see you Monday."
"I doubt that," she quips,
"today's my last day."

And then there are times
that are never fun.
When there is no room,
up stairs you must run.

After twenty flights
you get to your desk
and now you must take
ten minutes to rest.

Of course the strange smells
cause everyone to wonder;
who's responsible
for that social blunder?

A psychological
study of cases
observed test subjects
trapped in tight spaces.

What they discovered
was perfectly clear,
most people possess
a deep rooted fear.

Elevator ride,
face it or quit;
easing the tension
is the true test of wit.

Cube Farm

Spanning ten thousand square feet of space
are the individual workspaces of an industrious race;
the human employees, in a furious chase,
for the almighty dollar, while remaining in place.

Over the short gray walls their heads will appear,
like groundhogs questioning if spring is now here.
Some venture outside for a drink when it's clear,
then dart back in their holes when sensing a supervisor is near.

Of this sort, I confess, I'm a part.
The walls of my cube are cluttered with art.
And on the day of gladness when I finally depart,
I shall confess 'twas I who did silently fart.

My wife's cube is much deeper than mine.
The walls of her cube come up to your eye.
Thus taking a seat, you're fully disguised.
And the shadow of the cube blocks out sun and sky.

Walls so thin everyone can hear
the conversations you have with only one ear.
And if by chance it ends with a tear,
e-mail of condolences will start to appear.

In these part-time habitats, on the walls have been placed,
pictures and things of each individual's taste.
These sterile enclosures put up in such haste
are now personalized with our accouterments and waste.

Like a beaver's dam swept away by a raging stream,
my prized window cube that once allowed me to daydream,
was reshaped and reassigned to new departments and teams.
So now my only view consists of paper reams.

Facing a window is prime real estate;
when it's offered up don't hesitate.
Our need of escape is completely innate.
But it's being confined we're forced to tolerate.

When the day is over and the last shift is done,
the labor for one crew has merely begun.
For cleaning this quagmire is like a daily dump and run;
the humans come in and trash is hauled out by the ton.

Some consider these cubes a modern day wonder,
but in the design there's a structural blunder.
Because these life-sized Legos are thrown easily asunder
when employees leave the company and their cubes we can plunder.

Like a maze of gopher holes, or anthills, or beehives,
in a cube farm we may spend half of our working lives.
And every day, as we endure our morning drives,
it is for the window office we know everyone strives.

Desk Stuff

Awards and pictures,
books and postcards,
inspirational sayings,
calendars and candy jars;
there are some things that serve a purpose,
there are some things that explain who we are,
there are some things that keep us organized,
there are some things we brought from afar.

I've seen a piñata of a blue bunny,
I've seen an action figure of Sigmund Freud,
I've seen harmonicas and basketball trophies,
I know the cleaning crew's totally annoyed.
One day they will simply stop cleaning,
because of these things that get in their way,
creating more obstacles they must work around;
I expect they'll all trash them one day.

You have to wonder about certain people
who keep their desk free from personal clutter.
There are many who consider their behavior quite odd,
under their breath you will hear them mutter;
"She must be some type of clean freak,"
"He must be anal retentive."
The people whose desks that are kept the cleanest
are the people we deem most obsessive.

Model cars and comic book characters,
an aquarium and a Mr. Potato Head;
there are more stuffed animals around up here
than my daughter has home on her bed.
You'd think we just returned from a carnival,
or that we worked in a giant toy store,
and rather than seeing full grown adults
you'd see little children coming through the door.

There are steel balls in these little red boxes,
people say that they help them relax.

One nervous guy actually has two sets,
he claims he's prone to panic attacks.
And then there are balls that are much softer
that you're supposed to gently squeeze.
But I've blown out three of them already
from all the stress I've been trying to relieve.

Yes our desks are covered with trinkets
and collectibles of sentimental worth.
Some people literally have dozens of them,
you'd think they'd been collecting from birth.
So when we get into financial trouble
and all of our cost cutting is to no avail,
rather than laying off hundreds of employees
we should have a huge office garage sale.

The Coffeemaker

The impact of the coffeemaker
upon our history
has never been more profound
than on the office employee.

Around it-
we stand and wait.
Around it-
we procrastinate.

The coffeemaker is wise.
The coffeemaker gives life!

The responsibility is severe
for the one who comes in first
to brew a stiff black pot of verve
and slake our coffee thirst!

Around it-
we politic.
Around it-
we shall picnic.

The coffeemaker works late.
The coffeemaker is great!

Our wrath came down one day
on some fool who knew not
how to differentiate
the decaf from the caffeinated pot.

Around it-
we will revolve.
Around it-
our work will stall.

The coffeemaker is wise.
The coffeemaker gives life!

We never agreed on the protocol
of who's supposed to brew the joe.
Somehow it's all understood.
Innately we all just know.

So when you take of the last drop,
even if your cup's half full,
you'd better fill up the pot
or you'd better have some pull.

Around it-
we have to wait.
Around it-
we will gravitate.

The coffeemaker works late.
The coffeemaker is great!

The loudest complaints came
when the little baggies were no more;
"No coffee to make this morning?"
"Show office manager the door!"

We'll take a salary cut
perhaps even no AC.
But we all will quickly riot
if you suggest a coffee fee!

Around it-
we watch it brew.
Around it-
no work we do.

The coffeemaker's the key
To a happy employee.

Disgruntled Employee

Hair disheveled,
reeking of gin,
shirttail untucked,
bloody tissue on his chin;
he showed up today,
much to my chagrin,
he's the disgruntled employee
and I must manage him.

He blows up when confronted,
he scares everyone around,
he laughs at the shy girl
like some deranged clown.
He pounds on his keyboard
like he's stomping the ground.
He's one angry employee
and he never jokes around.

You hope that one day
he'll show up with a smile
and greet you with cheer
and relax for a while.
But joy just eludes him,
happiness not his style;
always mad as a hornet
and bitter as bile.

You tried to write him up
but he just laughed in your face.
Then yawped, "As a manager,
"you're a total disgrace!"
He'll fight tooth and nail
like he's running some race.
He's got his own agenda
and he won't be put in place.

Sometimes I swear
his eyes will turn red
when I simply correct him
over something he said.
I wish I could fire him
but I cower instead.
He's so damn intimidating
his reactions I dread.

I fear that one day
he'll show up with a gun,
snapping like a twig
that's been baked in the sun,
and start shooting at random
hunting co-workers for fun.
And since I'm his manager
I'll be the first one.

I asked him one time
to take a vacation
and he glared at me
with such great irritation.
"I have too much work!"
he barked in retaliation.
He has no idea the meaning
of insubordination.

He is disgruntled,
there is no doubt.
The question to me is,
"What is he disgruntled about?"
He gets paid well.
He has a little clout.
But when he opens his mouth
he seems to just shout!

He walks with his jaw clenched.
He grumbles under his breath
about the work environment
that will surely cause his death.
He'll ignore you if you say good morning,
of all pleasantries he is bereft.
He'd prefer to just spit in your face
if he has any spit left.

And when I simply call him,
I can feel his temperature rising.
I know that in his mind
it's his entire life he is despising.
Through all the madness and the anger
and all the relentless chastising,
finally his reign of terror has ended,
for his department is downsizing.

Always Late

Five minutes, ten minutes,
fifteen minutes, twenty;
her excuses for being late
we used to think were funny.

But when all the other employees
have to race and sweat;
showing up to work on time
is something she just won't fret.

Every day, it seems to be,
the traffic's worse for her than me,
or her alarm clock did not sound,
or she forgot it was turned down.

Today there was an apartment fire,
and yesterday she had a flat tire,
and one day when the roads were clear,
she wrecked her car trying to avoid a deer.

So twenty minutes, thirty minutes,
forty minutes, or fifty;
getting away with being late
is something she finds nifty.

When red-eyed employees have already arrived,
with coffee at screens they stare.
But the thought that's boring into their minds
is her empty cube and chair.

A few times she has turned around
once on her way to work,
going back home to change her clothes
after she spilled coffee on her skirt.

Another morning her cheap hair dryer
would not completely dry her hair.
She prattles on and on about her troubles
and we're just forced to grin and bear.

From fifty minutes, to an hour,
to an hour and a half;
at this point her lame excuses
are well beyond a laugh.

When single moms and family dads
can all get here on time,
for this particular individual,
it disturbs her peace of mind.

From late subways to rainy days,
whatever may make her late,
you think you've heard her best excuse
but tomorrow's will be just as great.

Her stories are now legendary,
her fables by heart we know,
her tall tales are ever expanding,
especially during winters without snow.

We never understood why she wasn't let go,
how she got away with it, and with such glee.
Until that day when she showed up with flowers
and an engagement ring from a Senior V.P.

The Breakroom

Put down your guard
you're in the breakroom,
so enjoy the conversations and scents.
It's best not to whisper or interrupt
but in here you can put in your two cents.

Communal freezer,
or perhaps even two,
cleaned out each and every week.
Previously it was every other month
or until the leftovers started to stink.

Some eat and read,
some talk or get coffee,
some check for doughnuts
left by other departments.
In here there are no worries; always plenty to do.
So kick your feet up, you're in the breakroom.

Pull up a seat,
get in on the scoop,
you will hear these things no other place.
Like who's dating whom, and who just got canned;
things we would never just say to their face.

Some come with games
like foosball or pool tables,
some may even have a little café.
But the best one that I've ever seen
contained six full size bowling lanes.

The great meeting place, all gather here,
for quick meals or the vending machine.
Sometimes we may even have birthday cake,
or decorate it with a seasonal theme.

Yes everyone's back in the breakroom
for happy occasions or just for a drink.
But be sure to clean and put away all your dishes
and please throw away anything that's starting to stink.

Vending Machine

They stand side-by-side in the breakroom
dispensing a variety of treats
to all the hungry employees
who forgot to bring something to eat.

Filled with chips and candy bars
and other enticing bait.
Most all employees have partaken
and put on additional weight.

There are health nuts that complain
about the vending machine.
But yet at the end of every week
the contents are completely picked clean.

Its convenience so alluring
to satisfy their hunger need;
they try to resist with all their might,
but eventually even the health nuts concede.

We couldn't understand the rumbling
coming from behind our wall.
Until we caught somebody rocking it
trying to get his chips to fall.

The Honey Buns are my weakness;
I'll consume the entire row.
And when the vending machine runs out,
to the convenience store I will go.

And when I forget my lunch
I can create an entire meal;
five thousand calories for just two dollars,
I consider that a pretty good deal.

One Friday I forgot my wallet
and could not access my snack.
So I waited around for the guy that refills it
to see if he'd give me one left on the rack.

He claimed he wasn't supposed to.
The owner, he said, really cares
about every single nickel he gets;
but then he slipped me some Gummy Bears.

There are some snacks that don't sell well
among the machines' selections.
Trail mix and salted almonds
are always passed over for other confections.

If it complements a cup of coffee,
or if it gives you a sugar high,
or if it works well alongside a sandwich,
we'll consume the entire supply.

So don't try to sell us your health food,
your rice cakes or any fresh fruit.
We'll raise cane with our facilities manager
and convince her to give you the boot.

We want our Oreo cookies!
We're not trying to get any thinner.
We just want something that can tide us over
until we get home and can have our dinner.

The Scavenger

He comes out when no one is looking
or when everyone's gone for the day.
He is not fond of cooking.
For his meals he shall not pay.

He loiters around in the breakroom.
The refrigerator is his trap.
All the naïve employees'
lunches are reduced to scrap.

He'll even open the door for you
so you can place your delectables within.
But as soon as he is alone in the room
his devouring begins.

You can never leave something frozen
with the hope that you'll have it later.
The smile that you see on his face
is that of an alligator.

Anonymity is his cover;
he never leaves a trace or clue.
But the theft that was most painful to me
was when he ate my wife's homemade stew.

I devised a plan to ensnare him
by leaving rancid meat with a stench.
But his stomach must be made of iron—
it seems nothing can cause him to wrench.

He reminds me of some type of fish
that lurks deep at the bottom of a lake;
anything that comes his way
he will very gladly take.

The scavenger is always prowling
for a quick meal left unprotected.
He'll nab it before you know it
and disappear undetected.

So beware what you store overnight;
trying to hide it is all for naught.
Although we have set many a trap
to this day he has never been caught.

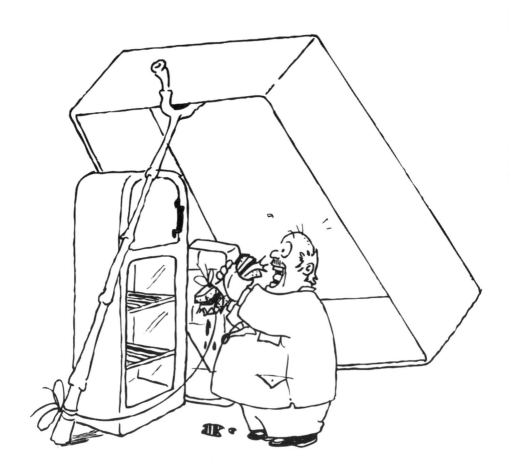

The Fax Machine

You check it every five minutes,
tense and nervous you feel,
as you wait for that huge contract,
or that important business deal.

You've secured all its wire connections
and increased the paper supply.
An e-mail simply won't cut it;
you must have a signed reply.

It's unequivocally integral
to the commerce of today.
So always remember to check the print cartridge
and refill the paper tray.

Transmitted through electronic voices,
its blinking eye indicates it's ready
to send your orders and invoices;
business is good when its workload is steady.

In this modern age of computers
we still need a signed contract,
because when someone sues the company
that signature may be only hard fact.

When it has problems we get angry;
nothing else can trigger such rage,
than when a sheet comes out all crumpled,
or with black streaks running down the page.

We know that telephones and computers
all have their parts to play,
but the fax machine keeps on working
long after we've left for the day.

It may hum and sputter,
squeak and grind,
but no matter its volume,
we don't seem to mind.

For as long as it's operating,
and our business can be done,
its chirps and high-pitched whining
are all just part of the fun.

Because a business is in business to make money;
but money's color doesn't come in just green.
Sometimes it's plain black and white paper
and it comes through the fax machine.

Paper Jam

Open the tray,
then give it a slam,
it's not out of paper,
it's a paper jam.

Lost in the spools,
clogging the gears,
there's a mangled page of work,
that usually results in tears.

Caught in its teeth
you tug a tattered edge;
but the rest of your precious document
is now acting like a wedge.

The blinking lights
indicate where to look;
to find the sheet that's been lodged
you must check within every nook.

Whose fault is it?-
That's just the way it goes.
Every copy machine acts up some time
and gets a kink somewhere in the hose.

Technology has evolved;
do you recall that disks used to be floppy?
Do you remember the days before the fax
or blue fingers from carbon copy?

But still no copy machine is resistant;
when it happens feel free to yell "Damn!"
Don't you dare try to avoid fixing it-
you're a victim of the paper jam.

Lunch Break

You take it at eleven
thinking you'll avoid the crowd,
but a client calls in
all frustrated and loud.
You work through his issues
and head for the door,
glancing at your watch,
it's 11:04.

You head for the elevator
while jingling your keys,
when a new hire approaches,
"Can you help me please?"
His lost puppy dog look
you cannot deny,
by the time you finish,
it's 11:09.

Into the garage
you must descend,
all eighty floors,
to meet your friend.
But he is not there
at the place you agreed.
Confused you just wait,
it's 11:15.

Leaving without him
you jog to your space.
Against the clock
you now must race.
A hasty lunch
you always rue,
the clock on the wall states,
it's 11:22.

You open the car door
in ephemeral bliss,

no lump in your pocket
tells you something's amiss.
You forgot your wallet,
it's in your desk drawer,
by the time you retrieve it,
it's 11:34.

You punch the accelerator
and speed from the lot.
When the gas gauge blinks on,
there's another thing you forgot.
When you left this morning
your tank was on "E".
When you stop to fill up,
it's 11:43.

Selections of restaurants
pass through your mind.
Only fast food chains
can serve you in time.
When you finally decide
on a place to dine
the bank sign displays,
it's 11:49.

You sit in your car
as you calculate the line.
When it's finally your turn,
you hear their chime,
"Welcome to McDonalds,
may I please take your order?"
You ask for the time,
it's 11:54.

Your situation now
is a hopeless fate.
For if you order your food,
you know you'll be late.
So you jump out of line,
like a madman you drive,
as the DJ yammers,
"It's 11:55!"

You screech to a halt
and race up the stairs.
The clock is still ticking
as you trip over chairs.
You make it in time
to plop in your seat.
Your lunch break is over,
but you never did eat.

Liquid Lunch

There's no better way
to break up your day
than the standard liquid lunch;

when quotas are due,
and the leads are few,
and you're really feeling the crunch;

the neighborhood bar
is not very far,
on some days it calls out your name;

when you are stressed out,
fidgeting about,
the remedy's always the same.

You leave sharp at noon,
returning at two,
you're "making some outside calls."

And when you get back,
they'll cut you some slack,
the top sales awards are all on your walls.

Your secretary's
your sanctuary;
your secret is safe with her;

she'll cover for you
with a wink and a "Shoo,"
confident her job is secure.

At your favorite place,
to ease the fast pace,
a stiff drink helps you calm down.

So loosen your tie,
but you don't have much time,
so order a double on every round.

Zipper Stain

In the men's restroom
there's a real dripper;
every time you flush
it sprays on your zipper.

I get a real laugh
when I see each patron
grab a toilet seat cover
to use as an apron.

While some people try
to quickly jump back;
it's not their speed,
it's distance they lack.

The force and pressure
create a small jet.
No matter how quick,
you're gonna' get wet.

Excuses are few
and difficult to fake.
Most people assume
you neglected to shake.

The first time I went
all the raves and rants
I had forgotten,
so it sprayed on my pants.

I felt like a fool
standing in there
just trying to dry
my crotch with warm air.

The suspicious looks
I inevitably got.
Like I was some pervert
who had just been caught.

And when I returned
my face was a blush.
I said to myself,
"Next time I won't flush."

Forget the manners,
don't leave it to chance,
unless you come to work
with a spare pair of pants.

Shared Restroom

A cry goes out to the forsaken ladies
forced into the most deplorable situation;
sharing the only restroom with the men of the office
is the bane of your personal sanitation.

The query arises with every visit,
"Who was the last to use the facility?"
Women are cautious when the lid is down,
and despise having to wipe the seat.

Their tender buttocks always uncertain
when nature calls them to take their seat.
But on the way down if they detect a small drop
they will stop in mid air and retreat.

There are usage signs left behind,
gender specific clues, that are tell tale.
Like a tampon wrapper on top of the trash
or a *Motor Trend* draped over the handrail.

Raising the seat and leaving it up
was once quite widely accepted.
Placing responsibility on the next user
to then lower and disinfect it.

But now that half the workforce is women
the duties have increased for each visit.
Today women expect a stain free toilet
and to sit down without having to touch it.

Men understand there are two motions,
forget one and your respect is diminished.
The first one is raise the lid before you go
and the second is lower it when you're finished.

No one is immune to the embarrassment
and the suspicion from a lengthy trip.
If you're not in and out in two minutes
with muffled voices you will hear some people quip;

"He sure has been in there awhile,"
"I hope he hasn't fallen in,"
"I hope he's not sick to his stomach,"
or "Is there a window we can open?"

I detest the false pride of finger pointers
who cast blame and arrogantly think
that of all the people in the office
it's their crap that does not stink.

Our circumstance is irreconcilable
unless we construct an outhouse.
Sharing a restroom with anyone is awkward
even if it's at home with your spouse.

So you women get over being timid
and if a foul odor causes you to blush,
simply light a match or spray air freshener;
you can always blame a man if you forget to flush.

Recognize My Shoes?

Oh no!
My stomach's foe,
a third cup of joe,
and a big grumble below.
This feeling I know,
never coming on slow,
gotta' go, gotta' go,
gotta' go, gotta' go.

Oh my!
I'm not like a guy,
I'm really quite shy,
but I'm not very sly.
Now my morning's awry
and I've gotta' fly,
gotta' fly, gotta' fly,
gotta' fly, gotta' fly.

My doom!
I fear the restroom,
the smell will loom,
while the women assume,
that I'm out of perfume,
gotta' zoom, gotta' zoom,
gotta' zoom, gotta' zoom.

Drive to
my home I must do,
to relax while I poo,
no one seeing my shoes,
I won't be accused,
as the woman who,
let a stinky poo, stinky poo,
stinky poo-poo!

Smoke Break

"Are you ready?" is all
some have to say.
Others just nod
and they're fast on their way.

Some go alone,
some in a pair,
wasting this time,
only non-smokers care.

The smell of their clothes,
the smell of their breath,
with every break,
quickening their death.

Sweating like pigs
or shivering in the frost,
they'll gladly have a smoke,
never mind the health care cost.

Each outside exit
on a building's bottom floor
cigarette butts litter
twenty feet from every door.

Forty years ago
you could smoke in any place.
But health codes now force
smokers to the alley in disgrace.

Behind a desk or
on the street broke,
to join their ranks just ask,
"Excuse me, do you have a smoke?"

Yes smokers stick together,
it's part of their daily routine.
So just let them have their smoke breaks;
take it away and they become downright mean.

The Dipper

No smoking in the office
may cause nicotine fits for some.
But not for the ones who like to have
a pinch between their cheek and gum.

When the stress seems overwhelming
or anxiety is high for the crew,
rather than having to take a break
a dipper will reach for his chew.

He smacks the can with fingers
with a skillful flick of the wrist,
signaling to all his peers
there's a loophole that they have missed.

No need to walk downstairs
to have a smoking break.
He's got his can already in hand;
a huge dip he'll proudly take.

The spit cups tend to offend
some who are weak in the knees.
Just be sure to give him plenty of room
in case he has to sneeze.

He knows he's getting away with something
that should not be allowed at work.
And underneath the lump in his lip
you can sense his mirthful smirk.

When the boss comes by he can hide it
by pushing it back in his jaw.
And if by chance he needs to spit
he'll use a cup with a lid and straw.

He knows it's truly disgusting,
that fact he won't debate.
But try to strip him of this pleasure
and this peaceful dipper becomes irate.

I wanted to see his reaction
so I hid his can one day.
But after looking for just one minute
he grabbed another he'd stashed away.

I'll never forget the time
he reached for a cup to drink
and swallowed a gulp of his left over spit
then bolted to puke in the sink.

He's aware that many will stare
or bicker and complain.
But he'll take a dip wherever he's at-
even next to a lady on a plane.

The spit cups line his desk
like little un-flushed toilet bowls.
He ignores all warnings and health concerns;
he'll continue until his lips have holes.

We tried to pass a no dipping rule
but there was something we did not know;
the biggest dipper of all at work
was our red-neck CEO.

So after lunch you'll hear the slaps
as the dipper packs his can.
The pungent smell we must endure
for on dipping there is no ban.

The Water Cooler

The cooler talk around up here
can cool your nerves
or burn your ears.

The snide remarks pour here at work,
to hear a jab,
around it lurk.

It's a common place to get the scoop,
the latest trash,
the deepest poop.

Found in the hall or the breakroom,
always near it
the rumors loom.

As people grab a cup to drink,
the water drips,
they start to think.

And then they dump as you walk up,
all their complaints
into your cup.

From it conversation flows
about the news
or TV shows.

All politics try to avoid;
there're always some
who'll get annoyed.

Religion is also taboo;
don't Bible beat
on that Hindu.

Don't get yourself into hot coals
by always trying
to save lost souls.

Cuss a manager, yours or mine.
But share your faith,
you've crossed a line.

The water cooler's where you can sink
into a mire
with just one drink.

Storage Cabinet

Put a sign that says "Free" next to something
and people will just come along and grab it.
And so the story goes with the office supplies
that are kept in the storage cabinet.

It's like a treasure trove of handy objects
that begs you to take more than you need.
When you see a supply of the pens you like
you'll sense that primal greed.

There is a threshold to the taking
the company doesn't consider as theft.
So when trying to calculate how many to take
make sure there are at least a few left.

I was anxious about the things I took
but my stockpile lost all attention,
after the CEO and several accountants
were caught stealing from the employee pension.

You may be lucky by the size of your company
to have more that just a storage bin.
I've seen converted closets or entire rooms
that cause all the employees to grin.

It's like seeing a full stocking on Christmas
or a bunch of presents stuffed under the tree;
with Post-it notes and spiral notebooks
and shiny staplers for all good employees.

I discovered some things are off limits
when the marketing manager got miffed
at a few employees that helped themselves
to some expensive promotional gifts.

These objects that help keep us organized
these fasteners and reams of paper,
these folders, envelopes, and rubber bands,
paper clips, glue sticks, and staplers,

are now the sole responsibility
of one person to maintain and restock;
in an effort to cut down on the pilfering
we must now sign out for the key to the lock.

Sick Day

Statistically speaking
a trend has been shown,
Friday's the day
most people stay home.

It's obvious to me,
the work week's too long.
Setting it up
we got it all wrong.

When Monday is second
for all absentees,
it makes more sense
to cut the work week to three.

We all use our sick days
except when we're sick.
But this one day vacation
requires a trick.

We can't work all five days,
we have things to do.
Like sleeping off
a cocktail flu.

Or improving our game
out on the golf course;
when you call in
just sound like you're hoarse.

Or going to the mall
to buy a new dress.
Or simply cleaning up
a six month old mess.

Or my main priority,
catching up on some sleep.
I need these ten hours
to work at my peak.

So one day's a sick day
out of the work week.
Declare it now!
Just stand up and speak!

When we all take a stand
we'll have much more free time,
and we can all put it on
the company dime.

Fire Drill

Oh yeah,
what a thrill!
Here we go
it's a fire drill!

Smokers stand up
and grab their packs;
the CEO jumps
through some escape hatch.

All sales reps
stay on the line;
it's just a drill,
you'll be just fine.

Security guard
grabs his light;
the nervous girls
start to push and fight.

Take those stairs
just down the hall.
Don't rush, don't run,
don't trip and fall.

Don't shove or kick
or you'll get hurt.
It's just a drill,
you won't get burnt.

Each employee
has a place;
just stand right up
and show your face.

Now count 'em up
each by name;
it's just a drill
but ain't no game.

There's somebody's
career at stake;
to him it's real,
to us it's fake.

Self-Evaluation

Once a year,
or perhaps even quarterly,
your supervisor will ask,
"Do you have your report for me?"
And you're reminded it's time
for managements' retaliation,
a process they call,
the self-evaluation.

It's the invention
of some HR guru
who has studied in depth
all human moods.
And thus set into motion
having to justify your promotion
by writing down all you've done for that year.

Yes spelling counts,
use specific examples,
ensure your calculations are accurate,
and be sure not to ramble.
Modesty?
Don't be naïve.
You must sing your own praise.
You've got only 2000 characters
to justify that 5% raise.

I find it quite amusing
that everyone who works here
is required to use it.
And when I am reviewing
my own performance
I still have to go over
my subordinate's.
While my boss gives his
to his supervisor,
this equalizer
spares only a few at the top.

Each department has
its specific criteria,
whether you work in management
or just the cafeteria.
Your quarterly review-
it is the place where you
get to brag about your talents and accomplishments.

There are those who take it
very serious.
They work on them until
they're delirious.
They keep revising and editing
so before the meeting
they're sweating it,
all because their goals were not met this year.

The slackers brush it off.
When it's mentioned
they'll scoff.
And afterwards they'll question
why they don't have a pension
and remain at the bottom of the trough.

So when it's time to rate yourself
and your words affect your wealth,
then don't withhold
any claim how bold,
your worth must be told,
in the spaces that seem all too few.

Please Micro-Manage Me

Please micro-manage me.
Make sure I dot my "i's" and cross my "t's".
I'm too productive when I think for free.
I need for you to micro-manage me.

When I take a step out on my own
please tell me where I need to go.
I feel inept when left alone.
Without you I'm just a drone.

When I come up with an original thought
please critique it 'til it's all for naught.
And tell me why it's doomed to fail.
You are the hammer that drives my nail.

Please micro-manage me.
For I am blind and cannot see
the huge mistakes that will surely be
in my work I submit to thee.

When I attempt to devise a plan
point out the risks that are at hand,
and all the costs we would incur
until I'm deflated and must concur.

At times when my goals seem clear,
please question me until doubts appear.
And raise concerns I'd not thought of;
please pick apart the ideas I love.

Please micro-manage me.
I'm like an errant ship that's lost at sea.
Your navigation is what I truly need.
Your brain is far superior indeed.

With my reports that I submit
kick them back without a hint
of what exactly must be changed
until a one-on-one can be arranged.

And when it's time for my review
focus on all the wrong things I do.
And criticize my disposition
or grill me like it's an inquisition.

I hope that soon there will come a day
when all red tape is stripped away.
But if you're fired or your position's phased out
I fear I'll have nothing to complain about.

Team Meeting

It's time for a huddle.
Morale is depleting.
Call the troops together.
We need a team meeting.

In the conference room at nine
for all is mandatory
and if you're going to be late
start working on your story.

It starts with some light banter
or some jovial wisecracks
to help lighten up the mood,
to help everyone relax.

The brownnoser will try
to impress us with his wit.
Until someone shuts him up
by calling out "that's bullsh.."

Then there are the know-it-alls
who chime in at every pause
to interject their wisdom
or point out strategic flaws.

To entertain yourself
observe the subtleties.
Some people have strange marks,
some act peculiarly.

Looking around you'll notice
people fidgeting about
some scribbling on notepads
or pulling a nose hair out.

A nervous tic, an ear pick;
now you're getting the gist.
A stained tie, a lazy eye;
what was that point you missed?

One guy is falling asleep
a girl is twisting her hair,
one guy is just daydreaming
and obviously doesn't care.

One nerd has buried his face
deep in some technical book.
The new girl is getting hit on
by a salesman with a horny look.

"All right people listen,"
you will hear the boss man say.
"I've got things to cover,
so cut out all the horseplay."

Just as you think he's breaking
into his well established routine
he throws everyone a curve ball
and pulls down the video screen.

Oh wow! This is exciting!
Maybe he's arranged some movie clips.
But once again we're all disappointed
as into slides of our sales stats he rips.

Well, the first ones were around a fire
and they drew on the walls of a cave.
But even in the team meetings of today you'll notice
how primatively some humans behave.

Top Salesperson

Women in the sales force
are completely changing the game.
Every company that I've worked for
the top sales rep was a dame.

Many of them have acquired wisdom
over the course of a few tough years,
and rather than their male counterparts
when they listen they use both ears.

Women make good mentors
who are willing to share their knowledge.
Some are great at motivating people
from being cheerleaders in college.

Some may be single moms
with infant sons and daughters.
Some are college educated,
some graduated with honors.

One thing's proven to be true,
salesmen can never rest,
because if your competing with women,
be prepared to not be the best.

If you managers can't figure out
why morale may be deflating?
If you're still pitching all salesmen,
it's time you bring in a saleslady.

If your male sales reps are slacking
and are in need of a kick in the ass,
go find a handsome woman,
a real determined lass,

who has to close sales
to pay this month's rent;
she'll sell in a territory
that the salesmen claim is spent.

She'll raise the bar,
(in more ways than one),
she'll give it her all,
until she has won.

But treat her fairly
and show her respect
or a sexual harassment case
you can surely expect.

If your sales results are lacking
no need to worry or fret,
you just probably haven't hired
the right saleswoman yet.

If however,
the top salesperson's a man,
be aware, that title
can quickly change hands.

Here is a fact,
a cause for reflection;
in last Sunday's paper,
in the real estate section,

in all of the top spots,
at the top of each board,
there was a woman who sold most,
and all women who got awards.

So top salesmen bask in your glory,
things can change by next year;
your manager could hire a woman
and to her we all may cheer.

Yes the times they are a changin' men,
so throw in your pink slip towels.
For if you're counting on a career in sales
be aware that most of the top reps are gals.

Blame Game

Everyone plays the blame game
because everyone's job is at stake.
From the client service rep to the CEO
no one likes to claim a mistake.

You push it around like a leaky bag
filled with human excrement,
and every time your name comes up
it's to your reputation's detriment.

The backbiting and the jeers
that shade and spin the truth
are now accepted as part of the culture;
things that were once considered uncouth.

Some people have become experts
at dodging the mark of the blame.
But trust in the fact that the truth shall come forward.
They'll have their dark day of shame.

Some people say you can cover a hole
but unless filled, you'll keep falling back in.
Or until someone honest comes along
who is willing to take the stripe for your sin.

For I've seen the biggest of shirkers
break down and turn over a new leaf
after someone noble took a hit for the team
and left all present in mute disbelief.

Once all the dust had settled
and we could focus on the solution
our fingers quit pointing in all other directions
and fueling this morale pollution.

So when it comes to blaming someone
and you feel like pointing the finger,
remember it's like wafting a smelly fart,
you're just helping it spread and linger.

Lateral Move

I'm not one hundred percent happy
with what I currently do.
I don't want to leave the company;
I'll try a lateral move.

There are jobs here that people envy;
there are jobs here that are much more fun;
there are jobs here with fancy titles;
unfortunately mine is not one.

I'll check the internal job postings
for a position of which I could boast
that does not require a pay cut
or that I move to the opposite coast.

I don't want to lose my benefits;
I just want to try a different groove;
I don't want to forfeit my tenure;
I want a lateral move.

I am not going to let anything stop me
except a high-pressure interview.
I believe if I just apply myself
there's something better right here I can do.

In a year I get a sabbatical
so changing employers is not all that wise.
It's not the company that I dislike
it's what I do that I despise.

I've outgrown my current position;
I have nothing left to prove;
I'd prefer a different avenue;
I'd prefer a lateral move.

This company is tremendously large.
Better opportunities await.
But sacrificing all my stock options
to me doesn't sound all that great.

I frequently think about my future
and I long for a prosperous career,
but I would really be disappointed
if I was still doing this in a year.

For me a lateral move is perfect.
I can begin to do what I want.
It's like writing the same e-mail
in just a slightly different font.

Next time I see a job open
I'll submit my resumé
and beg and plea and fervently pray
I get my lateral move one day.

Demotion

The bitter pill of demotion;
from the office to the cube;
the shortening of the title;
the stripping of the view;

the quickening of the senses
when the meeting takes a turn,
one you were not expecting,
it's now you whose gonna' burn.

It was wrong from the beginning.
You sensed it in your gut.
Restructuring always meant
some are let go and some take a cut.

They called it an opportunity.
They needed your expertise.
But in fact what they are doing
is chopping you down right at your knees.

The burning sting of demotion;
like a swift kick to the crotch.
No matter how they spin it,
it's to take you down a notch.

"We're paying you too much money,"
is the sentiment behind their teeth.
Everyone will benefit,
at least that's the company's belief.

They gave you some time to transition,
somewhat lessening the blow.
They told you to take a vacation.
Some place relaxing you should go.

When all of the dust has settled
you'll easily slide back in.
You'll assume a brand new role.
New projects you can begin.

It ended with a handshake
as they deftly pulled out the knife.
You bit your tongue as you begrudgingly thanked them
for train-wrecking your plans on life.

The blatant stripe of demotion;
you wear it as best you can.
You knew the risk when you started this job-
it comes with working for the man.

A Raise

At the office it is honest to say
that there are rarely few better days
than the ones when you come in unsuspecting
and found out you've gotten a raise.

The boss' hand you will get to shake.
You'll receive a few pats on the back.
You thought this day would never come—
please refrain from your heart attack.

Your time at work is worth more today
than it was just a day before.
Your past performance deserves recognition
and your threat to leave we couldn't ignore.

We've conducted a thorough analysis.
Management knows you don't have to stay.
In the labor market your skills are in demand
so we've decided to raise your pay.

It took some consideration
but we're convinced it's money well spent.
We took the standard rate of inflation
then tacked on about ten percent.

So take your wife out to celebrate!
Go buy that new car you wanted.
But we'd prefer it wasn't obvious to co-workers
so around the office try not to flaunt it.

Or else they too will come 'round asking
for their salaries to also be raised.
And management would have to continue to do that
until it's the same amount we all get paid.

Brownnoser

His day is filled with cheerful glee.
He has little work or responsibility.
Yet, he is paid twice as much as me.
You'd think he was a V.I.P.

He knows just when to make his move;
when client calls are backed up in queue,
or when several customers begin to gripe,
the boss' butt to him looks ripe.

He's always holding a coffee cup
to wet his lips while sucking up.
All the favor of the boss he soaks
by repeating to him his banal jokes.

His obsequiousness cannot be hidden.
It is with the boss that he is smitten.
His loose tongue has been known to blame.
He'll freely gossip and show no shame.

Several times a day you'll see him there
in the boss' office without a care.
It does not matter when others stare.
He relies on the fact that life is not fair.

True talent he does not have.
To call him valuable is a total laugh.
It's fairly easy to perceive
that his life is filled with insecurity.

His sappy nature drives us insane.
Why the boss can't see it, we can't explain.
He must be blinded by the glow
of all the compliments from him that flow.

Whenever there is an important crowd
you'll find him closely loitering around.
Then from his lips his charm will ooze;
he's a master in the art of schmooze.

While others all work hard to succeed,
working hard to him there is no need.
He need only wear one dirty hat;
it's kissing ass that he's best at.

Loudmouth

She is just plain loud.
She talks as if shouting over a crowd-
of twenty thousand.
She is just plain loud.

Her laugh makes you deaf.
It's louder than the whistle of a ref-
through a megaphone.
Her laugh makes you deaf.

She screams at random.
Her conversations are a pandemonium-
of cackles and gaffs.
She screams at random.

Her voice is a bull-horn.
Just a few words and her welcome is worn-
like nails down a chalkboard.
Her voice is a bull-horn.

She has got giant lungs.
From her mouth harsh phrases are flung-
like someone's banging on a drum.
She has got giant lungs.

She cusses all day.
Without swear words she'd have little to say.
Her laugh sounds like a jackasses' bray.
She cusses all day.

She is just plain loud;
like a thunderstorm in a dark cloud.
She could incite a riotous crowd.
She is just plain loud.

Facilitator

He's there when things are happening
of a somewhat serious nature.
He's a master of explaining things.
He's the facilitator.

When things get a little too heated
and people need time to back off,
we need someone to calm us down;
someone who eats from a different trough.

When there's friction between employees
he supplies the much needed grease.
His effeminate nature works well
in reestablishing the company peace.

Arbitration is his forte;
he'll pacify confrontation.
He'll allow everyone time to explain themselves
and he'll clarify any obfuscation.

His soothing and sensitive words
and his politically correct degree
qualify him as a specialist
at putting conflicting parties at ease.

When sometimes things just happen
which result in people not getting along,
his position always seems to be
that no one is actually wrong.

All opinions are very important;
compromise is the key.
He is the facilitator
and he's goal is for all to be pleased.

Personal Assistant

Personal Assistant
have you no shame?
Living your life
for another's gain;

having no freedom,
tied by a chain,
doing petty chores,
feeling disdain.

Personal Assistant,
attached to a name,
of someone important,
or someone of fame.

Break out on your own
and be your own boss;
you can reclaim
the identity you've lost.

Personal Assistant
you can take charge
by burning all
your business cards.

Just sever your reigns
and run like the wind.
This act of liberation
they can not rescind.

Personal Assistant,
one step away
from the big player;
planning his day.

Pay off the lien
that's been placed on your soul.
Take back your life
from whom it was sold.

CEO

He's at the top of the corporate structure.
His name all employees should know-
because it appears on all their paychecks.
He's the company CEO.

He may drive a red Ferrari
or he may drive an old Ford.
He affects the future of many.
He sits at the head of the board.

He's like some mythical character
of which legends are told.
His house is a sprawling mansion.
He's worth more than his weight in gold.

He's the captain steering the ship.
He's the conductor of the symphony.
He can be remembered as a hero
or he can go down in infamy.

The great ones know their customers
and reward their employees.
The bad ones buy their own jets
while ransacking the company.

They can make other people wealthy
or become utterly corrupt.
But they still get a hefty bonus
even if the company goes bankrupt.

Some are street smart and down to earth;
some have only paper knowledge;
some started their business with an inheritance;
some in their dorm rooms while at college.

No matter what their upbringing
or the education they received,
it's apparent that when you get paid too much money
even the most upright person can be deceived.

Important company announcements
are recordings of his voice.
He sells us the new corporate vision
as if we ever had a say or a choice.

It's touching when they take a salary cut
to show the public that they are willing
to help the company get out of a glut;
to them ten million is just a few shillings.

I used to let out a belching guffaw
when some customers would try to name drop,
and when I couldn't resolve their issues
they'd boldly demand to speak with the man on top.

To this ultimate superior,
only the most important decisions should go.
His shower-curtain's worth more than my wife's wedding ring.
He's the company CEO.

If you ever get to shake his hand,
think before of what to say.
You have one shot to make an impression
that he'll remember beyond that day.

So tell him your name and your talent,
your insight and your intention;
tell him about your biggest career dream
or your brilliant new invention.

You just might catch a willing ear
that has deep pockets to grease the wheel.
He just might tell you to give him a call
to work out a business deal.

So don't write them off as all evil;
they're not all like Mr. Lay.
These men and women of great power
can help you achieve your dream some day.

Well, "The bigger they are, the harder they fall,"
or so the saying goes;
and so, "The higher the climb, the further the fall,"
is my proverb for all CEOs.

Gamer

You began with *Shoots and Ladders*
and its partner *Candyland*,
but you quickly discovered that compared to electronics
board games were simply too bland.

In your quest you discovered Atari
and in a day you aced *Combat* and *Pong*.
Soon you desired better graphics and challenges
and upgraded to Nintendo and *Donkey Kong*.

The grip of your addiction
tightened along with your age,
spending thousands on cutting-edge technology
in order to keep up with the gaming rage.

And on your sixteenth birthday
you turned down a new motor scooter.
While your parents stared at you baffled
when you asked for this thing called a computer.

Your first job was at Radio Shack
and your free time was spent in the arcade.
You asked your boss if, instead of a check,
in quarters you could be paid.

And once you did have a girlfriend
which lasted almost a week.
Until she confessed she could not take the pressure
of being seen in the halls with a geek.

Right now your hair is so shaggy
your face can barely be seen.
Next month you turn thirty two
but you behave as if still just a teen.

You're a wizard with things
that must be plugged in.
You're a master of games,
you won't stop 'til you win.

You're a gamer, oh gamer,
your hands move with such speed.
You could have been a rocket scientist,
but you like to smoke too much weed.

Spam

Damn the spam,
curse the spam,
block the spam,
except for one,
and then it grows
just like a weed,
until your inbox is jammed.

Spam, spam,
damn the spam!
Damn the spam to hell!

It wastes your time
day in, day out,
it makes you cuss,
it makes you shout.

The war is on,
firewalls set up,
our daily work
it will interrupt.

Spam, spam,
damn the spam!
Damn the spam to hell!

Prescription drugs
and mortgage rates,
miracle ways
to lose some weight,

hi-tech addicts
running a scam,
pushing their junk
through billions of spam.

Spam, spam,
damn the spam!
Damn the spam to hell!

Your e-mail address
was put on some list,
you click "remove",
they still persist.

An internet solicitor
got it with ease,
and inundates you
with e-mail of sleaze.

Spam, spam,
damn the spam!
Damn the spam to hell!

It ticks you off
with each e-mail;
it makes you scream,
it makes you yell.

Delete, delete,
'till your finger's sore;
the misleading titles,
you can't ignore.

Spam, spam,
damn the spam!
Damn the spam to hell!

"Need a lover?"
Just click right here.
Fifty prospects
will now appear.

"Manhood too small?"
Realize your dream
by clicking on
this podsy scheme.

Spam, spam,
damn the spam!
Damn the spam to hell!

"Stock trades for less-
we'll make you rich!"
Give us your money,
ignore the hitch.

A credit check
we'll run for free.
An "unsubscribe"
means nil to me.

Spam, spam,
damn the spam!
Damn the spam to hell!

A millionaire
we called a geek,
created his wealth
by spamming each week.

In his garage
computers abound.
In all his spam
I wish he'd drown.

Spam, spam,
damn the spam!
Damn the spam to hell!

A "No Spam" list
to him's a joke;
his solicitation
has no yoke.

Hiding behind
a fake address,
trying to reply
creates more stress.

Spam, spam,
damn the spam!
Damn the spam to hell!

I used to like
to get e-mail.
Now my system
runs like a snail.

I never buy
a single thing.
My rage surges,
with every "ding"!

Spam, spam,
damn the spam!
Damn the spam to hell!

Some even have
a nasty worm,
or some strange type
of computer germ.

Of all the spam
I hate most,
the virus spam
that serves as host.

Spam, spam,
damn the spam!
Damn the spam to hell!

So damn the spam!
Curse the spam!
Block the spam!
Outlaw the spam!
We will reclaim
our e-mail inboxes.
Release the hounds!
Let's hunt spammers like foxes.

Spam, spam,
damn the spam!
Damn the spam to hell!

Workstation

Before the advent of computers
I believe it was called a workspace,
but it morphed into its current name
about the same time the typewriter was replaced.

Every morning upon arrival
a gamut of steps we must replay
to correctly log into a computer
so it can show us our "To Do's" for the day.

We all complain about long hours;
of the expanding work day we bemoan.
Some employers even refuse to pay you for time
that you're not logged into your computer and phone.

Some managers get nice peripherals
like speakers or a twenty-one inch flat screen.
But only the highest ranking employees
are granted a dedicated line and fax machine.

Don't use it for surfing the internet,
or playing some computer game.
Personal use is strictly prohibited
that's why "work" is the first part of its name.

When combining "work" with "station"
its meaning becomes quite apropos,
because once I'm finally logged into it
there are few other places I'm apt to go.

Webster describes it as, "a person's work area,
including some sort of computer."
But going from a corner office to a cube farm
wasn't exactly covered by your last recruiter.

Frustration is easily triggered
when some administrator has had to log in
and neglects to switch back your user name and password
creating a memory challenge before you can begin.

We've broken down our parent company
into hundreds of various departments.
Now all incoming letters will be lost
unless it's coded for a specific compartment.

Every workstations has been assigned a number
in case you must relocate within the cube farm.
Some people have covered theirs in stickers
to give it some character and charm.

Yes the workstation is the essential tool
that keeps track of every move we make.
I've even seen them calculate the time
each employee wastes while taking a break.

The Day the Internet Went Down

Surfing with ease
from page to page,
through the internet hole
we escape from our cage.
Just burning away
half of our day
by shopping online
and chatting away.

When quite suddenly,
while engaged in solitaire,
pop up warnings
on my screen did appear.
Then someone yelled,
"I just lost the internet!"
Next, my screen flashed blue
and away my connection went.
One of my best games,
ranked in top place,
was now forever adrift
in cyberspace.

I then began to worry
about my personal identification.
Did I neglect to close that web page
with all of my credit card information?
And what about those customer accounts
I was just laboring on?
I don't think I saved my changes-
that's another hour's work just gone.

This freakin' internet!
It's slow and choppy and freezes.
It seems like it looses connection
every time someone near the router just sneezes.
We recently switched back to cable
after we tried switching to DSL.
We thought it would speed up our connection
but instead it just gave us all hell.

You then see running down the hall
a nervous new I.T. guy.
You can tell by his expression
something's gone terribly awry.
He shouts out to everyone,
"Everybody just reboot!"
As we all retort in unison,
"We already did, now what, dude?"

He then gets swept up
like a hairball in a broom
by some level two I.T. guys
rushing to the server room.
Without any further excuse,
without any further ado,
he tucks his pride and silently exits
trying to salvage his damaged repute.

How am I supposed to work
with a computer and no internet?
How am I supposed to check e-mail,
or chat with that chick I just met?
How I am supposed to find out
the latest on Angelina and Brad Pitt?
How am I supposed to stay current
on what celebrity couples just split?
How can I get through my day
with no Google or YouTube?
Do they actually expect me to focus
on the work here I get paid to do?

Irate Customer

It maybe his first time to call in;
she may have done this before;
one thing's for certain, you can tell in their voices,
their scathing calls you'll come to abhor.

He has no intention of listening;
she did that for an hour on hold.
The light jazz intended to sooth them failed,
so the first person that answers they'll scold.

Monday I had a peeved housewife call in
at first so upset she could barely speak.
But after I said, "Please try to calm down."
She exploded and cursed a blue streak.

It is futile to try and appease them,
with their frustration don't try to relate.
This rancor's been boiling for some time in their stomachs
and has turned these customers irate.

They'll interrupt all helpful suggestions
with degrading snubs making you feel inferior.
They'll cuss you out and before you can talk back
they'll demand to speak to your superior.

One hacked client locked me in his crosshairs
and figured out my direct extension.
Making my life as miserable as his,
it seemed was his sole twisted intention.

In this fast paced world of technology
people get furious when the must wait.
The software or computer they once loved
is transformed into an object of hate.

No matter how belligerent they are,
if your pay is tied to their satisfaction,
carefully select each and all words
most unlikely to cause a reaction.

As you endured one customer's eruption,
you daydreamed about the beach in Cancun.
And when he exclaims, "Are you listening?"
You press hold to punish him with another tune.

You take some minutes to gather your wits
and go through a little troubleshooting.
In silence you can research the issue,
while placed on hold, he is left brooding.

So when you punch him back into your line
after giving him some time to relax,
you can't even get a word in edgewise;
on you he's determined to grind his ax.

But in one brief moment of peace
after his hour long tirade of terror,
an apologetic tone came over his voice
when he realized it was all user error.

Whether it be e-mail or over the phone
your situation can quickly worsen.
At least you don't have to work at some store
where you may be forced to handle one in person.

An irate customer is plain tough to deal with,
but remember, life isn't always about fun.
Virtually all human beings at some point in their life
have lost control and turned into one.

Monday

There's something very wrong with Monday;
that's a fact on which we can all agree.
More horrendous things throughout time
have occurred on this day of the week.

Whoever first said, "I hate Mondays",
expedited its demise.
Because from that Monday until now
it has brought many a bad surprise.

Perhaps you have heard of "Black Monday,"
the start of the Great Depression.
The stock market crashed and banks went bust,
not the best of first impressions.

You'd think we would have learned our lesson,
but several other crashes thereafter,
even if stocks rallied on Friday,
Monday brought total disaster.

More keys are lost,
more wrecks occur,
more employees call in,
it's cursed we're sure.

We argue more,
more flights delayed,
this weekday hex,
just won't go away.

The worst time to book an appointment
that's cursed with impending doom
is not the late time slot on Friday,
it's anytime Monday before noon.

You can always blame it on Monday
if you're late, or sick, or just down.
No need to say more, we all understand,
on this one day it's acceptable to frown.

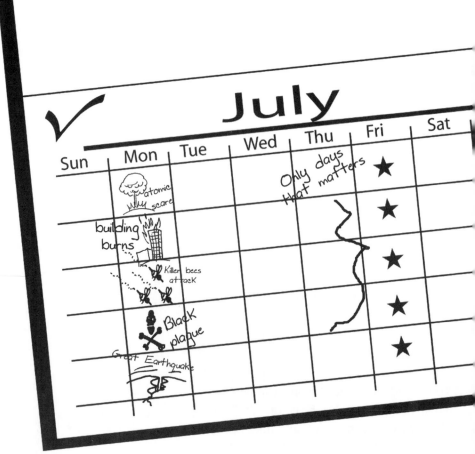

July

Sun	Mon	Tue	Wed	Thu	Fri	Sat
	atomic scare			Only days that matters	★	
	building burns				★	
	Killer bees attack				★	
	Black plague				★	
	Great Earthquake				★	

Office Punks

Perennially exceeding the boundaries
of the appropriate office wardrobe,
her pink hair and black fingernails
make all who see her say, "Whoa!"

Nowhere in the employee handbook
does it address such severe cases,
such as, what types of tattoos are acceptable on employees
or how many rings are allowed in their faces.

Her boyfriend works in the mailroom
and has a chain from his nose to his ear.
But it's not his freakish looks that repel me,
it's his fiendish stench which I most fear.

His flimsy wife-beater t-shirts
reveal a mosaic of charm;
freely dispersing his odor,
while displaying the art on his arms.

They meet together for smoke breaks
and talk about comic book characters.
In rags they sip on café lattes'
and crush all attire-related barriers.

The day she showed up with her pet,
everyone first thought it was fake.
Until she pulled a mouse from her purse
and proved it was a real live snake.

On one calm Monday morning,
in a neck brace her boyfriend did arrive;
with a laugh and a wince he chortled,
"No one caught me on my stage dive."

The Sex Pistols, The Misfits,
Black Flag, and The Clash,
all appear on their T-shirts;
but their true love is Johnny Cash.

They light up the office
like living lava lamps.
They get a steady paycheck
while dressing like tramps.

Yes the office punks keep the workplace exciting
when our attire seems drab and gray.
Office Punks we hail and adore you!
What will adorn you today?

Office Affair

It was trouble from the very start;
that we all knew.
Business relationships are usually kept cordial,
but not for these two.
Although he was married
the attraction between them grew.
It was an inter-office affair
they decided to pursue.

Her conservative attire
began to change.
Her skirts started to cover
a more limited range.
Their secretive nature
to everyone seemed strange.
Like special meetings together
that he would arrange.

The looks and the smiles,
the touching of his arm;
her flirtatious nature
encouraged his outward charm.
They were just having fun,
they didn't mean to cause harm.
He told us to not worry,
there was no real cause for alarm.

On the day they both called in sick,
eyebrows were raised.
At their audacity
we all were amazed.
For his integrity
he was never praised.
They were hungry to become lovers;
for only each other they craved.

The company parties were awkward
for all who came,
when he arrived with his wife
to try and cover up his shame.
But none of us were fooled;
he couldn't hide the blame.
His exploits are renowned-
hunting women like wild game.

One day it came to a head
his wife came home early
and caught them in bed.
The secret was out!
The romance was dead.
The excitement replaced
with embarrassment and dread.

Justice was swift in the office.
We all had plenty to say
about sexual harassment cases
popping up every day.
So he was moved to another department
with a ten percent cut in pay.
Both reputations were tarnished
and have not recovered to this day.

I've heard old timers squawk,
"Don't crap where you eat."
And although it sounds vulgar,
that bone still has some meat.
For every time I see it happen,
the results always repeat.
So keep your love life outside of the office
and use the head that's furthest from your feet.

Workaholic

You've seen him before
with his rolled up sleeves.
He's the first one at work
and the last one to leave.

The bags under his eyes
have been deepening for years.
He can only operate
in the highest of gears.

He drinks coffee like water.
He's up before five.
There is no end
to his motivation or drive.

No one can outwork him.
He has no social life.
He'll sleep in his office.
He's on his third wife.

His desk is a war zone.
His briefcase is battered.
His life is a wreck.
His nerves are tattered.

He's climbing the ladder.
Over many he's stepped.
Don't try to compete;
you'll just look inept.

He'll take every task
that happens his way,
completing them early,
without extra pay.

If it's not about work,
he simply won't care.
He's worked so damn hard
he's lost all his hair.

He's got no time for small talk;
he prefers to just wave.
He'll never retire.
He'll dig his own grave.

He works every Saturday
and Sundays as well.
To him life without work
would be like living hell.

He won't take a day off
for a vacation or flu.
He'll work from his bed;
more work he must do.

He pushes himself the hardest
like the lead dog of the sled.
He's usually been working for hours
while I'm still at home in bed.

Evading rest and enjoyment,
it seems work is all he needs.
Every day he arrives early
but on his way he still speeds.

He's burning the candle
at both ends of the wick.
In twenty four years of employment
he's never once called in sick.

The man's a machine
that knows not how to fail.
To keep him from work
you'd have to lock him in jail.

This is the workaholic;
get out of his way if you can.
He's on the fast track to destruction.
He's been brainwashed by the man.

Sales Call

Now sharpen up,
get on the ball,
closing sales takes
a good sales call.

They see your face
or hear your voice
but either way
they'll make a choice.

You try to get
on their good side
but all signs say
"Access Denied."

You sense the no
just by their tone,
if in person,
or on the phone.

Some interrupt
with a sharp quip;
at you they want
to lash their whip.

They feel cruel joy
in being rude.
They don't know you're
a righteous dude.

So shake them off,
move down the hall,
the next sale comes
on your next call.

Receptionist
at the front desk
catches your glance
at her large chest.

Her annoyance clear
at your presence.
She'd rather choke
than be pleasant.

Some people have
been taught to hate
the salesmen that
knock at the gate.

Perhaps one time
in childhood years
the saw their dad
reduced to tears,

weeping behind
his closed front door
wanting goods he
couldn't afford.

Or standing on
the porch one morn
with his fist raised
and words of scorn.

Barking at the
salesman that day
for messing up
his dirt driveway.

When making calls
in face-to-face
be sure to take
a can of mace.

Even by phone
or just outbound
there still are ways
to hunt you down.

Quota

In our first meeting
they touched on it a bit;
the quota that I
was expected to hit.

The number at first
seemed to be such a breeze.
With my sales background
I should hit it with ease.

But when I started
making sales calls,
the grip from my quota
was tight on my balls.

My first month I missed
by a single sale.
The next month I tried
to no avail.

The third month I thought,
it's in the bag.
But cancellations came
and created another snag.

For the first quarter
I was far from my goal.
I desperately needed
to get on a roll.

So in the fifth month
I tried a new angle.
But the incorrect paperwork
created a new tangle.

The sixth month I knew
what I needed to do;
I'd make more calls
and the sales would ensue.

By the seventh month
it was right in my grip.
But on the last day
through my fingers it slipped.

So on the eight month
my calls were more drastic.
But the clients complained
that I was too bombastic.

My ninth month arrived
and found me frustrated.
Even though I tried,
my will had abated.

So by the tenth month
my savings were gone
and all my excitement
was replaced by a yawn.

The eleventh month
updating my resumé
was my primary task
for my few remaining days.

My one year review
at the end of this month
occupied my thoughts;
I hit quota not once.

But in that meeting
I was quite amazed
to see my quota
not lowered but raised.

My manager said,
"You don't have to fear.
Not even top reps
hit quota their first year."

I'm still in the ring
hunting for elephants,
making tons of calls,
while riding the fence.

The pressure is fierce
in boiler room sales.
At the end of each month
I am walking on nails.

When your job depends
on hitting your quota,
if you miss it you get
not one single iota.

Company Bonus

We have a company bonus
but the structure some say is unfair.
Which always seems to be the case
when employees are forced to share.

The numbers are so confusing
you need an advanced math degree
to complete all of the calculations
and figure out what it'll be.

I tried to work through it one time
to plan my expenses that month.
But all it really accomplished
was making me feel like a dunce.

It starts off with an estimate
that's based on a certain forecast.
The first attempt I tried to make
differed greatly from the last.

Several percentages are used,
different for all departments.
You plug them into some sort of matrix
that has several more compartments.

There's a lot of rounding off involved
that will throw the numbers askew.
And numerous lines of very fine print
that you must carefully review.

Then there's a certain "X factor"
depending on your manager's opinion.
For he decides on the final payout
to all the serfs under his dominion.

Once I figured a handsome bonus
soon realizing the numbers were funny.
And then I crunched them all again
which showed I owed the company money.

After the taxes and retirement contributions,
all the deductions I did crunch,
the final amount left over
just barely covered my lunch.

Then there are the stranger cases
like one time I got a check twice.
And when I admitted I had I cashed them both
the payroll rep wasn't exactly all nice.

Some people always feel shortchanged
when they finally receive their check.
Like a card player with a lousy hand
claiming the dealer never shuffled the deck.

The company bonus structure,
I know I'll never figure it out.
And no matter how much the checks are for
always expect some people to pout.

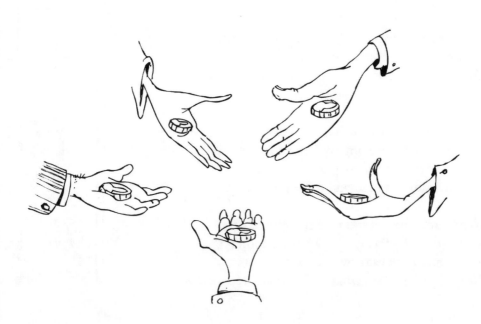

Company Stock

Between phone calls and business meetings
you've traded it and taken beatings.
It's up one moment then falls like a rock.
Your frustration is with your company stock.

You own it in your 401K plan;
buying it all when only up it just ran.
And when it tanked, your order to sell
did not get entered before the closing bell.

The college plan you had for your daughter
is all of options now underwater.
To retire early you played it smart,
but now your plan is to work at Wal-Mart.

Dollar cost averaging they said was the key,
but that was of little help when the price plunged to three.
You've seen your net worth fall to a number
that haunts you at night as you struggle to slumber.

When earnings are due you shake like a leaf;
beating the forecast the only relief.
And when the good news is finally announced
people still sell it in copious amounts.

Rather than paying my bonus in cash
they gave me more options to add to my stash.
So rather than buying something today
they delay any reward and force me to stay.

Yes there's one question we share together,
more frequently than, "How's the weather?"
It can fill the elevator with all kinds of talk.
Just simply ask, "So what's up with the company stock?"

Blue Blazer

A fading on the elbow,
some dust across the shoulder,
she's not the best looking jacket you've got
but she's steady as a boulder.

When success and drought
came and went
like the ebb and rising tide;
and the suits you had
that seemed to fit
now seem to creep and ride;
the blue blazer has stayed steady
so reach for her with pride.
Good 'Ol Blue, you get the nod.
Now let's take the world in stride.

The sleeves are cut to shake a hand
and display your choice of watch.
You can use her to dress up some jeans
or to take a suit down a notch.

When the liquor flows
and your wallet's fat,
and your bullcrap's thick,
as is your back,
'Ol Blue stays true
like a solemn pact;
no matter the scene
you'll stay relaxed.

She may be part of some suit
if you can still fit into the pants.
And so long as they've been altered
since your high school homecoming dance.

The new suits may come
when your fortune increases;
the better labels,
the sharper creases,

the most current of style,
from the neck to the shin,
as 'Ol Blue waits on a hanger
or in some laundry bin.

She'll hang for her night
to shine once again.
'Ol Blue is never offended
like some ideal friend.

The new suits will fit tight
when you've gained a little fat,
and 'Ol Blue will be remembered
when you forget the laundromat.

For the business may come,
other suits may be many,
but 'Ol Blue will be there
when you don't have a penny.
Or in the ninth inning
when all others are worn out,
just bring in 'Ol Blue,
she's clutch when it counts.

Well the first time you met her
may be a distant past,
or a new first experience,
but one that will surely last.
So whatever the occasion may be;
a graduation or ceremony,
formal dance or wedding party,
or some woman you've been courting.
You may have several suits
but not all will be ready.
Except for 'Ol Blue;
the one and only Blue Blazer.
So put her on and go rock steady.

Casual Friday

Back in the distant past
men would wear suits and ties.
But not long after the internet boom
the dress code went horribly awry.

The problem was exacerbated
as more women made up the workforce.
Permitting the dress code to include short skirts
put more curves in its historically straight course.

As conditions and standards eroded,
forgotten were jackets and ties.
And now with all the carpal tunnel syndrome
some men can't even zip up their flies.

I've seen warm-ups and baseball caps.
I've seen running shorts and even tank tops.
If the employees' clothes get any rattier
we may have to hire some dress code cops.

Now sandals and shorts are acceptable.
Tattoos and piercings abound.
Rarely among even top management
can a suit or sport coat be found.

Facial hair of all shapes and patterns
that you were once required to groom,
now grows so freely in all lengths and sizes
that it looks like a pirate costume.

One rainy day the men were titillated
by the secretary who was known to flirt.
After she forgot to bring an umbrella
and was tightly clad in a white t-shirt.

They say that fashion repeats itself,
even if once considered a fad.
So hold onto those parachute pants
and that leisure suit in red plaid.

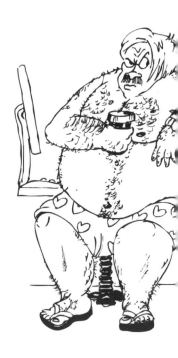

The dress code has been thoroughly butchered
with holes and loose standards to meet.
I've even seen the customer service reps
meandering through their cubes in bare feet.

What was once considered a privilege
is now accepted as the norm.
But if employees continue to push the limits
we may all be forced to wear uniforms.

This once only Friday occurrence
cracked the dam and started the leak.
Loosening the dress code on just one day
created the epidemic that is now casual week.

Office Mom

Dedicated to Katherine Rosella McKinney:
9/10/1921 – 3/31/2006

Her son is her boss when she lets him.
She welcomes you with her warm face.
She may smile as she hands you some candy,
but just as quickly she'll put you in place.

With tight fists she runs the front desk.
And with her spare time she mops the floor.
With toothbrushes, Comet, and grandchildren at her side;
if you don't smile she'll show you the door.

She types fairly well
and can answer the phone.
Better her be here
than alone at home.
Everyone likes her,
some out of fear.
More often than once
she's ripped them a new rear.

Don't dare be late on your payments,
it's not the boss who'll be making the call,
but the little sweet lady who answers the phone
who now sounds like she's fifty feet tall.

It's "yes ma'am" and "no ma'am"
when you answer to her.
When she offers you her cookies,
take them for sure.
And when the office lunch
is her home cooked favor,
you tell her it's wonderful
when it has no flavor.

Her eyes sparkle with charm and cut like a knife.
She types the bosses' letters while cussing his wife.
She'll make you some coffee that's not too bland;
no rudeness allowed, or she'll scald your hand.

She parks in the front in her own special place.
She wheels in her Buick, not a care on her face.
If you take it from her she'll throw a huge fit;
no one has been killed but a few have been hit.

Don't get me wrong, she's the most caring of persons.
But get on her bad side and your life only worsens.
One smart-alecky comment and all the damage done.
And for the next six months it is you she will shun.

She's lost two husbands,
the first in the war.
She's sharp a tack,
but soft to the core.
Her take on life,
an optimistic view;
her motto is,
"There's always something new
to look forward to."

Her service was rendered a number of years
and through these times she worked blood, sweat and tears.
Always staying busy while saving her pay
to give back to her sons as inheritance one day.

Company Christmas Party

'Twas the night before payday when all through the office
not an employee was working, nor were their bosses.
The computers turned off, all of the doors locked,
in hopes that at five it's out we all clocked.

The janitors were let off for the holiday cheer,
while in the mail, bonus checks began to appear.
And my wife in her best dress and I in my suit;
this company Christmas party was a knee slappin' hoot!

A drunken manager fondled the breast of some chick,
then goosed her girlfriend and thought it was slick.
Then what to my wandering eye should appear,
was the HR rep and his boyfriend Pierre.

With screw drivers and shots, Champaign and cold beer,
this company party was kickin' in high gear.
The head secretary went braless and we all did the train,
as the boss worked the mike and called us by name;

"Now Johnson, now Parker, now Peters, now Dodson,
on Sanders, on Douglass, on Palmer, on Watson,
belly up to the bar, let's all have us a drink,
because on Monday we return to our jobs that still stink!"

And then with the clashing of all of our glasses
the big boss did joke, "I've fired all your asses!"
We were all in rare form; yes some more than others.
Enemies in the office were now hugging like brothers.

Some women smoked cigars and hung with execs
and a couple got caught in the kitchen having sex.
We violated every rule in the HR handbook;
this year's Christmas party was completely off the hook!

Next Monday we spoke all about what had occurred;
the rumors were rampant while our memories still blurred.
Reputations were tarnished and damage inflicted;
so racy were the photos they had to be restricted.

Home Office

No more hunting for a parking space
or every morning having to shave your face.
No more fighting traffic
or putting up with the racket,
when you home office you set your own pace.

No more having to wake up early;
you can now sleep until noon or 'til three.
That is unless
your house is a mess
or your wife starts calling you lazy.

The first week started off great.
You got to sleep in and stay up late.
It was like you were taking
a temporary vacation
or back in school enjoying spring break.

But the bills continued to arrive.
So you mustered your will and your drive.
You set the alarm clock
and the automatic coffee pot
to prove you can still get up at five.

Upon waking, into excuses you delve
and recall your first meeting isn't 'til twelve.
You want some more sleep
so on the alarm clock's first beep
you knock it clear off of the shelf.

Some numbers you needed to crunch
was delayed because it took until lunch
to find your stapler
and your label maker
and to locate your only hole punch.

You thought it would help you concentrate
but the vacuum cleaner now makes you irate.

As does the washing machine
and when the doorbell rings
announcing the delivery of another huge crate.

Your office which started all clean
now gives you a sharp pain in the spleen.
Papers clutter your desk,
boxes up to your chest,
so now you can barely see your computer screen.

Yes there can be many benefits
when your home is also your office.
But don't expect to relax,
you can still get the ax,
and never forget who the real boss is.

Ode to Client Service Representatives

"Thank you for calling our company.
Can I please have your user ID?"
Please tell me all of the trouble you're having.
Please dump your problems on me.

Although you may not appreciate it,
not many customers do,
I am a fully licensed registered representative
and it is my job to cheerfully serve you.

I must know all your software applications
and each of their idiosyncrasies.
As well as our myriad of policies and procedures
that seem to continue into infinity.

So feel free to yell and scream and swear,
my tone will put you at ease.
And whatever tirade you throw my way
it is you I aim to please.

You shout at me, "Are your servers down!"
Because you can not log in.
You have no clue who your ISP is;
let the troubleshooting begin!

Now this client is a bit agitated,
and this one's being short,
and this one is so extremely pissed off
that he's threatening to take me to court.

"Sir I understand you are upset
and you don't have the time to chat.
But we don't provide support for their software
you'll have to call Microsoft for that."

They scream, "When will this problem be fixed?
When will this issue go away?"
My reply's the same as it was a month ago,
"I'm sorry there is no ETA."

"Yes sir, you might have a point there;
you can call me a dunce or a slack.
But as for now that's just the way it is,
so please refrain from your verbal attack."

"Sir I don't know what the e-mail said
and I don't know who you spoke to last.
But there is one thing that I can verify for sure,
this conversation is going nowhere fast."

At times I dream of being promoted,
or moved to a non-client facing department,
where I can relax at work and talk to friends
as if I'm on my couch in my own apartment.

I dream of starting my own business
and retaining all the profit and power,
and creating a really cool web page
as I sit in some luxurious tower.

I know I'll never be the highest paid here
or even employee of the year.
But my loyalty is regained every month,
when management springs for a keg of beer.

And yet in the midst of all the angry callers
there is the occasional client who knows
all the terrible abuse that I receive every day,
all the verbal jabs and blows.

And he takes the time to stop and say,
"I appreciate all that you do.
I realize you have a very tough job
but you've earned my trust and respect too."

"You are the only reason I stay with this firm.
You are the reason it is the best.
You are the most friendly and knowledgeable client service rep.
You are head and shoulders above all the rest."

The Walk

I once saw a movie,
I think it was called,
The Lords of Discipline.

And in it there was
a scene in which
a soldier who'd committed some sin

was forced to walk
out to the gate
while backs were turned by friends;

a statement that said,
we know you no more,
and you can never return here again.

Some years since then
I joined the ranks
of an army much different than him.

But in it there was
an HR policy
that seemed to be just as grim.

The look in their eyes
is petrifying
when you see the hatchet fall.

I can still hear the talk
from behind their cupped hands;
I believe they called it-"The Walk".

Most don't expect
the impending doom
that gathers from afar.

And then there are those
who know it's coming
because someone tipped them off in HR.

It starts with a pat
on the shoulder and that
is the tolling of the bell.

And then the polite
"Please come with me
We have something to you
we must tell."

"No, no, no need
to gather your things,
we'll send someone for
your stuff."

"Just come with us
and walk calmly this way.
You know we don't want to get rough."

"It's easier this way,
it truly is;
you've been a really good sport."

"But the lawyers say,
if we didn't do it this way,
you could sabotage us or take us to court."

And when he stood up
and shut down his workstation,
everyone's eyes started to shift.

As he was forever
separated
by a permanent and invisible rift.

It couldn't have been
five seconds or more
before they all started to swarm;

like vultures they came,
ripping things from his desk,
while his computer was still warm.

And when it was done
not a thing remained;
everything they did take.

And now his cube
is the locale
where we slice up the birthday cake.

How terrible it was
to see "The Walk".
It is something I'll never forget.

But when it's my time
they better come prepared
because it's a day they're gonna' regret.

The Interview

My resumé got me the call,
the call got me the show,
the show's my ticket in,
to the interview I go.

It's been about a year
since I last put on a suit.
Somehow it feels appropriate
when it's my own horn I must toot.

The shoes that I must wear
pinch and cramp my feet.
I'll wear them for one kind of person-
that person I now go to meet.

I ironed my shirt last night
and hung it up with care,
but my seatbelt was too snug,
so it got wrinkled on the drive there.

When he first approached me
his look shifted from my eye
and critically detected
the stain I'd not seen on my tie.

I gave him my best handshake;
a solid response my wish.
But that hope was quickly destroyed
for his grip was like a dead fish.

Once we were past the greeting
I didn't like the way he began;
he asked me to sit down,
yet he preferred to stand.

He paced around the table
and lectured me like a child.
The more that he explained the job
the more he got all riled.

I gave him my resumé
and he just tossed it on the table.
"I glanced at that already last night,
it's quite an entertaining fable."

"So let's just cut to the chase.
Why don't you tell me what you're like?
Your sweaty palms and wrinkled shirt,
suggest to me you rode here on your bike."

"What is your greatest weakness?
What gives you motivation?
Why would you be good at this job?
I sense some desperation."

"Why did you leave your last job?
Or were you terminated?"
His derogatory questioning
felt like I was being berated.

"I've gotten some good experience,
but I believe it's time to move on.
I work for an internet company.
It's here today but tomorrow may be gone."

"I'm motivated with a positive attitude.
I'm looking for a stable company,
that has a favorable compensation plan-
basically I want more money."

"I'm sure you can tell I work hard.
It's all there on my resumé.
I already know what you think I'm worth
so tell me what you're willing to pay."

We went back and forth for a few days
negotiating a starting salary.
But by the time we worked out all the terms
it appeared they wanted a dowry.

"You're actually overqualified.
We don't need someone with that much knowledge.
We prefer to hire someone with less
like a student straight out of college."

"We've found that it takes them longer
to realize their being underpaid.
We can work them for three additional years
and keep them on the same pay grade."

"We thank you for interest.
Have you thought of going back to school?
You know that being overqualified
is the exception not the rule."

Index

About the Author - Acknowledgements

The man is either mad, or he is making verses.
- Horace, Italian Poet, BC 65-8

Another profound statement from an era long ago is, "a poet is born not made." That insightful saying that elevated the status of a poet to that of a respected artist was later changed by a proud poet in the 1600's to state even more profoundly; "a good poet's made as well as born." That saying seemed to be the first one that differentiated between good and not so good poets. However, this version of the saying was altered yet again to, "a good poet is born and not paid", reflecting the current market conditions of the artform. This saying lasted for awhile but was then later upgraded to the more modern adage of; "a paid poet is good and not boring, reflecting public sentiment and expectations of poetry. However, the latest version of the saying now goes; "a poet is bored and underpaid". This is the most current version (5.0) of the saying to be used for this job application for Published Author.

Job Application for Published Author

Name: Robert Joseph Petta

A coonass!? I hear people born in LA are wild.

Birth Date: July 15, 1972

City of Birth: New Orleans, LA *Is this necessary?*

Status: Alive

Occupation: Writer/Poet/Performer

Home: Austin, Texas

Do people actually graduate from 8th grade?

Education

Grade School: Trinity Valley **Location:** Fort Worth, TX

Status: Graduated 8th grade **Year:** 1986 *I'm sure this is helpful to know*

Areas of Study: Literature, Music, Art, Latin

High School: Pascal High School **Location:** Fort Worth, TX

Status: Graduated: **Year:** 1990 *Oh Boy, we've got a Prima Donna on our hands*

Honors/Awards: Football Letterman 2 yrs., Baseball Letterman 3 yrs. Drama Club, Annual Staff, Young Life

College: The University of Texas

Location: Austin, TX

Status: Graduated **Year:** 1996 **GPA:** 3.0 *Can we verify this?*

Degree: B.S. in Communications *Great! a degree in bullsh...!*

Honors/Awards: Kappa Alpha Fraternity *Frat Boy (probably a salesman)*

UT Silver Spurs *a creative (wild)*

Creative Advertising Program *B.S. even better!*

Employment History

Company: Centex Destination Properties, Centex Homes Inc.

Location: Austin, TX

Position: Real Estate Sales at The Hollows on Lake Travis

Title: Sales Executive *— A salesman, I knew it*

Years: Oct 2006 - Mar 2007

Reason for Leaving: Change in life goals *What are life goals?*

Company: Lexis-Nexis, a division of Reed Elsevier PLC

Location: Austin and San Antonio, TX *He dealt with lawyers? must be thick-skinned*

Position: Direct IT Sales to Lawyers and Law Enforcement

Title: Sales Executive

Years: Oct 2003 – Oct 2006

Reason for Leaving: Change in career goals *— This is vague!*

169

Company: CyberTrader, a division of Charles Schwab
Location: Austin, TX
Position: Manager and Customer Service Representative
Title: Priority Access Manager, Senior Client Services Rep
Years: Mar 2000 – Oct 2003
Reason for Leaving: Change in income goals

Glorified receptionist

- money grubber?

Company: Morgan Stanley, formerly Dean Witter
Location: Dallas, TX
Position: Stock Broker, Financial Services
Title: Financial Advisor, Retirement Planning Specialist
Years: Oct 1996 – Oct 1999
Reason for Leaving: Change in location goals

Boiler Room churner?

- He moved

Company: The Southwestern Publishing Company
Location: Nashville, TN
Position: Direct door-to-door sales of educational books
Title: "Bookman"
Years: Four Summers 1993, '94, '95, '96
Reason for Leaving: Location, less travel desired, sold in over five
            different states, TN, MO, PA, KY, W VA

ever see Deliverance Squeel Boy!

Skills/Talents
Sales: Direct Sales, Business to Business Sales
Marketing: Direct Marketing, Direct Advertising, Copywriting
Writing: Poetry, Novels, Songs, Short Stories, Screenplays
Music: Harmonica, Guitar, Drums, Vocals

Drug test all musicians!

Interests
God, Family, Dogs, Music, Travel, Scuba, Reading, Running,
Boating, Biking, Cooking, Eating, Wine, Napping, Sleeping, Poetry

Poetry last? After napping & sleeping? I Don't know about this guy

170

Resume of the Illustrator
MARK SEAN WILSON

OBJECTIVE

To let the readers know, in brief, who I am and what I bring to *Office Poetry*. I hope to entertain the masses of many different business world gurus and those who would like to escape the world of office politics.

— What are gurus?

EXPERIENCE

Jan 1971- Ongoing   My Life   Earth, USA

Thank God a confessed terrestrial Carbon based lifeform

— Caps   *Double Trouble*

Was born in Los angeles, CA as a twin in 1971 to mother Nancy and father Ellis. My role was to grow up and work as a team player with my twin brother, Mike. My responsibilities include: developing my art skills from the age of 4 on up, receive my GED, graduate from Platt College school of graphic design in '02, married my beautiful wife Sherrie in '04, witness the birth of my son, Hayden Thomas Wilson in '06 and move to Austin, Texas in '07 where I would eventualy meet author Robert Petta.

;

Who is this? am I supposed to know?

→ What happened here?

obviously an Illustrator & not a writer

EDUCATION

— Repeat! (typos)

- **Grammer School- Edison Elementary School 1976-1983**
- **Junior High- Luther Burbank 1983-1986**
- **John Burroughs High- 1986-1989**
- **College Platt College 2000-2002**

Drug test all artists!

SKILLS

- Proud father of
  Hayden Thomas Wilson
- Loving husband of
  Sherrie Wilson
- Brother of 3 brothers
  (Oldest brother, Wayne, Older
  brother Scott, twin brother, Mike)
- Pen and Pencil Illustrator
- Digital Illustrator

— check with wife

- Graphic designer
- Digital photographer
- Movie buff
- Wannabe athlete
- Should-have-been poker player
- Die hard S.F. 49er fan
- Sushi consumer
- Harry Potter reader
- Picking up around the house

Aren't we all

Mr. Mom?

Comments

I sincerely hope that *Office Poetry* brings you great laughter and many chuckles for years to come, or at least while you're still working. These poems are the culmination of over 15 years of experience and my observations of the corporate work environment. Although many of the people, situations, articles, and themes in *Office Poetry* are based on actual events and individuals, any resemblance to people or companies living or existing, now or in the past, are purely coincidental and highly possible.

The intent of *Office Poetry* is not to discourage employees from working to their highest potential or to stir up rancor for being employed or in a position that is perhaps not your dream career. Rather, it is intended to help relieve all members of the labor force the daily stress and frustration that result from job related activities. It is for members of the workforce at all levels of employment from the janitor to the CEO to take an exaggerated and even distored glimpse of the the daily tasks and personalitites of those around them. It is intended to bring everyone to an understanding, that no matter what you do, or how hard you work, your attitude in life determines the ultimate outcome.

When reading *Office Poetry*, I feel confident you will be entertained, amused, and even enlightened by these observations in their poetic form.

Thank you,

Robert Petta
Author and Creator

Acknowledgments

Stephanie:	For standing by me, believing in me, and encouraging me through so much craziness
Savannah:	For being such a wonderful child of God
Dad:	For providing me wisdom and wit
Mom:	For instilling in me the zest for life and to dream
Nick:	For helping me keep the child alive inside
Candace:	For your prayers and spiritual encouragement
Roger:	For your love of reading and life
Nick Coppolo:	For being a great life coach and mentor
Chad Darbyshire:	For holding me accountable
Paul Fershstand:	For also enriching my sense of humor
Todd Hindman:	For building me up when I was down
Kaiser Malik:	For holding my efforts to the highest standard
David Newton:	For enriching my sense of humor
St. Clair Newbern:	For helping me with the music and sound track
Cheryl Nims:	For editing, critiquing, and correcting (the book)
Ron Nims:	For entrusting me with your daughter's security
Derrich Pollack:	For demonstrating what great things a man can do with his life if he follows The Lord's calling
Mark Wilson:	For all your hard work and hilarious drawings

Great Hills Baptist Church: For being our church home and family
The dedicated men of JTW: For reminding me to stay in the battle
My past employers: For providing me with life enriching careers
And the most important of all, my Lord and Savior Jesus Christ for forgiveness and eternal life. All praise goes to Him.

Light Underground and Office Poetry support Charity:

10% the net proceeds from the sale of this book as well as any and all other products from Light Underground Publishing and Office Poetry are donated to selected charitable organizations. For a list of the charities supported by Light Underground Publishing and Office Poetry, please visit the website at: www.officepoetry.com.